W9-ALJ-196

WITHDRAWN

Let Freedom Ring

The Jamestown Colony

by Gayle Worland

Consultant:
Julie Richter
Project Manager
Virtual Jamestown
Virginia Center for Digital History,
University of Virginia

Capstone press
Mankato, Minnesota

Capstone Press
151 Good Counsel Drive, P.O. Box 669, Mankato, Minnesota 56002
www.capstonepress.com

Library of Congress Cataloging-in-Publication Data
Worland, Gayle.
    The Jamestown Colony / by Gayle Worland.
    p. cm.—(Let freedom ring)
    Summary: Follows the struggles and triumphs of the colonists who came to the
New World and founded Jamestown Colony in what would become Virginia.
    Includes bibliographical references and index.
    ISBN 0-7368-2462-6 (hardcover)
    1. Jamestown (Va.)—History—17th century—Juvenile literature. 2. Virginia—
History—Colonial period, ca. 1600–1775—Juvenile literature. [1. Jamestown (Va.)—
History—17th century. 2. Virginia—History—Colonial period, ca. 1600–1775.] I. Title.
II. Series.
F234.J3W67 2004
975.5'02—dc22
                                                          2003013904

Editorial Credits

Katy Kudela, editor; Kia Adams, series designer; Molly Nei, book designer and illustrator;
    Scott Thoms, photo researcher; Eric Kudalis, product planning editor

Photo Credits

Cover image: Colonists landing at Jamestown, Getty Images/Hulton Archive

Corbis/Bettmann, 19; Tim Wright, 35
Courtesy of the Association for the Preservation of Virginia Antiquities, 36, 38, 39
Getty Images/ Hulton Archive, 9, 11, 13, 14–15, 17, 20, 23, 24, 26–27, 29, 31, 42, 43
National Parks Service/Colonial National Historical Park, 5
North Wind Picture Archives, 6
Richard T. Nowitz, 41

1   2   3   4   5   6   09   08   07   06   05   04

Table of Contents

Chapter One

A Time of Discovery

In December 1606, Captain John Smith and 107 other men left England and sailed across the Atlantic Ocean. They arrived in Virginia in April 1607. About three months later, many of the men were dead from disease. Many others were ill. Smith knew the group's food supply was running low. The men were **starving**. Something needed to be done.

Smith and a group of men set out to explore the area. Smith hoped to fish in the James River. But stormy weather kept them from catching any fish.

Smith's other plan was to trade for corn with American Indians. As they traveled by boat down the James River, the group came upon an Indian village. The village of 18 houses was spread out on 3 acres (1 hectare) of land.

Trade with the American Indians helped to save the Jamestown settlers from starving. The Indians traded food in exchange for goods.

At first trading began slowly. In exchange for a small ax, Smith and his men received a few pieces of bread. They also received small handfuls of beans and wheat. Smith would not give up. He returned the next day in hopes of trading for more food. This visit proved useful. Smith and his men received fish, oysters, bread, and venison.

On the journey back to the fort, Smith's group met more American Indians. These men, returning

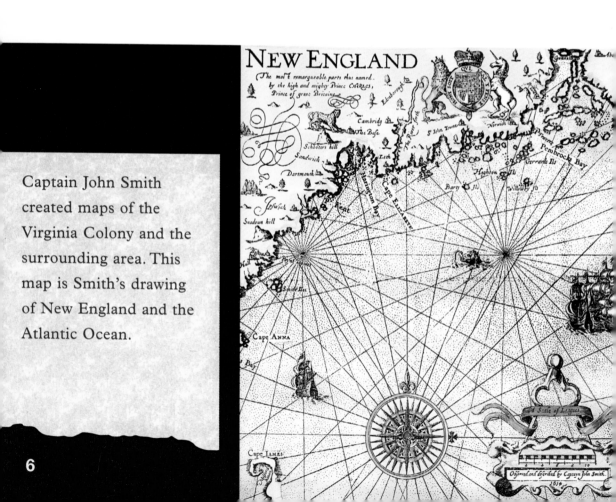

Captain John Smith created maps of the Virginia Colony and the surrounding area. This map is Smith's drawing of New England and the Atlantic Ocean.

from a hunting trip, also wanted to trade for goods. Smith traveled to their village. There he loaded his boat with corn. These exchanges started a trading relationship with the American Indians.

Smith Helps Jamestown

Smith is often credited for saving the Jamestown settlement. During his travels, Smith established a good relationship with the American Indians. Soon, American Indians traveled to James Fort to trade with the colonists.

Smith's leadership helped the colony grow. The colony of James Fort became known as Jamestown. Soon, the colonists added more settlements and formed the Virginia Colony. The Virginia Colony was the first permanent English colony in North America. Jamestown was the capital of Virginia for most of the 1600s.

Smith wrote eight books and many letters about his experiences. He also helped make maps of the new colony. Smith hoped this information would bring more colonists to Jamestown. Today, Smith's writings have helped historians learn about life in Jamestown.

Chapter Two

Founding Jamestown

John Smith and the other settlers sailed from England to make their fortunes. They rode on three ships, called the *Susan Constant,* the *Godspeed,* and the *Discovery.*

The explorers sailed from London with the blessing of King James I. England was tired of watching Spain grow rich with gold from new land. King James I granted a **charter** to a group called the Virginia Company of London. This group hoped the explorers would send gold and other goods back to England.

On April 26, 1607, the ships stopped along Virginia's coast. The passengers arrived at Cape Henry. This spot was located on the south side of Chesapeake Bay.

In May 1607, the English explorers sailed up the James River and settled their colony.

Choosing A Location

The three ships sailed up the James River into Powhatan Indian territory. In May, the men settled 36 miles (58 kilometers) upriver from the Chesapeake Bay. The settlers named their new home Jamestown in honor of England's King James I.

The explorers believed they had found a perfect spot. They could tie their ships to the trees in a nearby deepwater channel. The site was also hidden from unwelcome visitors. Within just a month after they arrived, the colonists built a wooden fort. They built James Fort to guard against American Indians and other invaders.

Struggles in Jamestown

Life in Jamestown was difficult. Many troubles seemed to strike the settlers. The food they brought from England spoiled. Rats got into the colonists' corn supply on the ships.

The location for the colony was a poor choice. The area was mostly swampy land. Swarms of mosquitoes carried deadly diseases.

A lack of food and fresh water also made many of the settlers ill. The following spring, only 38 of the original 108 men had survived.

Luckily for the surviving settlers, a ship from England arrived in October 1608. This ship brought more supplies and settlers. The total population of Jamestown grew to 120.

The first year in Jamestown was difficult for the settlers. Many died from disease.

Earlier Colonies

In 1585, English explorer Sir Walter Raleigh sent two ships to sail to the Virginia area. These colonists landed on Roanoke Island. This island was located off what is now the North Carolina coast.

These settlers built the first English colony in North America. The settlers quickly ran out of supplies. In 1586, all but 15 of the men returned to England.

In 1587, a group of 117 settlers arrived on Roanoke Island. Led by John White, this group hoped to find the 15 men who stayed behind. They planned to sail north together to Chesapeake Bay. But the men had disappeared.

Instead of traveling to Chesapeake Bay, the new settlers built a colony on Roanoke Island. A few months later, White sailed back to England for supplies.

A war between England and Spain kept White from returning until 1590. Upon his return, White found a deserted settlement. All White found was the word "Croatoan" carved on a tree. Roanoke became known as the Lost Colony.

The disappearance of the colonists is still a mystery. Some people believe a disease or American Indians killed them. Others believe the colonists went to live with the Croatan Indians.

Relationships with the American Indians

The Jamestown settlers had many dealings with the Powhatan Indians. Chief Powhatan ruled a group of about 30 tribes in the Chesapeake Bay area. This group of tribes was called a **confederacy**.

The relationship between the Powhatan Indians and settlers was mixed. Sometimes they fought and other times they traded peacefully.

The Jamestown settlers and Powhatan often traded with each other.

Pocahontas Helps Jamestown

Pocahontas was a daughter of Chief Powhatan. She became an important friend to the English colonists. As a young girl, Pocahontas often visited Jamestown. She brought gifts of food to the starving settlers. Captain John Smith believed she helped save the colony. Pocahontas helped to create friendly relations between the Powhatan Indians and the English colonists.

But relationships changed between the settlers and the Powhatan. In 1613, Pocahontas was captured by the English and brought to Jamestown. During this time, Pocahontas became a baptized Christian. She received an English name, Rebecca.

In 1614, Pocahontas married John Rolfe, a
leader of the colony. Two years later, she visited
England with her husband and infant son.

Pocahontas was baptized
a Christian. She was
given the name Rebecca.
John Gadsby Chapman
completed this painting
in 1840. Today, his
painting *Baptism
of Pocahontas* hangs
in the U.S. Capitol.

Chapter Three

Settlers Face Difficulties

Many of the first settlers in Jamestown were English gentlemen. In England, gentlemen hired servants to work for them. They were not used to taking orders or working hard. Many did not know how to build shelters or how to grow food. Most of the men were only interested in finding gold and silver.

Captain John Smith took control of the colony. He learned the Powhatan language. He asked the Powhatan for corn to feed the settlers.

In September 1608, Smith was elected president of the colony. He knew there was much work to be done. Crops needed to be planted, and better shelters needed to be built. Smith quickly set strict work rules that required everyone to work. "He who does not work, will not eat," Smith said.

The Jamestown settlers learned to build shelters.

In 1609, an injury ended Smith's leadership role in the colony. One night along the James River, Smith was camping with a group of men. A spark ignited a pouch of gunpowder on his belt, and Smith's clothes caught on fire. He was badly burned. Smith was carried back to Jamestown and soon sailed on a supply ship back to England.

Troubles in a New Land

The Virginia climate was a challenge for the Jamestown settlers. The settlers were not used to the hot summer weather. Many of the settlers also were not healthy when they arrived in Virginia.

If summers were bad, winters were even worse. The winter of 1609–1610 became known as the "starving time." The settlers did not store enough food for the long winter ahead. Then ships arrived with more settlers. These ships brought only a small amount of food supplies. Most of the food was rotten.

Many of the settlers did not live through the winter. By early summer in 1610, the few settlers still alive decided to abandon Jamestown.

Captain John Smith

On the day before his 28th birthday, John Smith boarded the *Susan Constant* bound for Virginia. Smith had already lived through many adventures. At the age of 16, Smith left his home in England. He became a hired soldier. Returning to London after four years, Smith was fascinated by stories of the land found in Virginia. He decided to invest in the Virginia Company of London and join the explorers on their journey to Virginia.

Smith made some enemies on the ship while crossing the Atlantic Ocean. At one point, he was put in front of the ship's "court of **inquiry**." Smith was accused of causing trouble on the ship. The court sentenced him to be hanged as soon as the ship reached land. Fortunately for the rest of the colonists, Smith's name was later cleared. Smith would become an important leader at Jamestown. He served as the colony's president in 1608 and 1609.

The settlers boarded a ship and headed down the James River. On the way, they met a messenger. This man carried a letter from the new Jamestown governor arriving from England. Lord De La Warre ordered the settlers to return to the colony. Many were not happy to go back to Jamestown.

In the next months, Lord De La Warre helped bring some order and success back to the colony. He ordered the residents to clean up Jamestown.

Jamestown grew into a successful colony. The settlers worked hard to build a town within the walls of James Fort.

By 1611, the settlers had created a town within the walls of the fort. The town included two rows of houses, a two-story storage bin, a church, and three storehouses. In 1612, more colonists and livestock arrived on ships from England. Many of these new colonists built other settlements along both sides of the James River. They kept Jamestown as the capital of Virginia Colony.

Damage to the Powhatan Population

These English settlements caused problems for the Powhatan. The settlers tried to take Powhatan land. Battles quickly broke out.

An unknown number of American Indians were killed in battles with the colonists. Only the settlers left a written record of their struggles. Historians can only guess at how many American Indian lives were lost in battles with settlers.

A 1646 treaty would later force the Powhatan Indians to give up their claims to land. In return, the Powhatan received a reservation on the north side of the York River.

Chapter Four

Making a Living in Jamestown

As the colony grew, the settlers tried to produce goods that could be sold in England. They needed to find products that they could grow in Virginia. Their attempts at making silk and growing grapes failed.

Jamestown's biggest moneymaker was tobacco. In 1612, John Rolfe brought tobacco seed from the Caribbean island of Trinidad. He crossed the native Virginia tobacco plant with the Trinidad tobacco. Rolfe created a sweeter-tasting tobacco that people smoked.

Virginia's rich soil was good for growing Rolfe's tobacco. Farmers soon began planting tobacco on large farms called **plantations**.

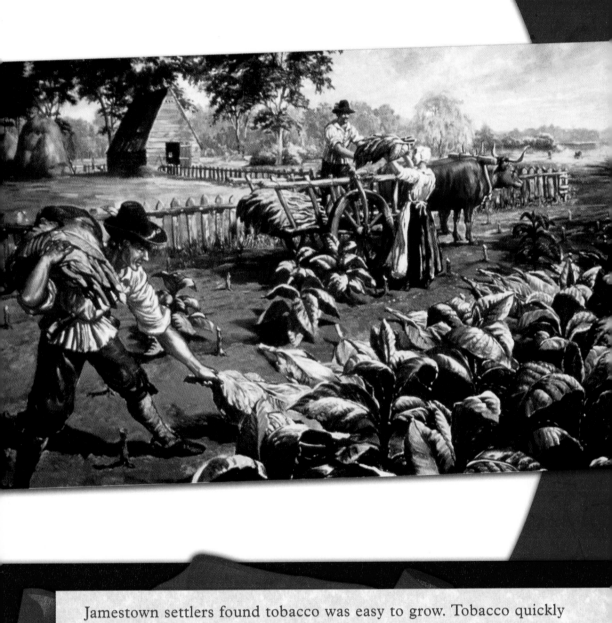

Jamestown settlers found tobacco was easy to grow. Tobacco quickly became Jamestown's most important crop.

John Rolfe and Tobacco

    The English cargo ship *Elizabeth* sailed from Virginia on June 28, 1614. This ship probably carried barrels with the first of John Rolfe's tobacco. Rolfe was a clever planter. He crossed the native Virginia tobacco plant with a sweeter tobacco found in Trinidad. Rolfe's tobacco saved the colony's business.

Rolfe's tobacco was harvested and shipped to England. Soon, tobacco became Jamestown's most important **export**.

Glassblowing and shipbuilding were some of the colony's major industries. The colonists sent many items to England to be sold.

An Important Year

The year 1619 was important in the history of Jamestown and the colony of Virginia. The Virginia Company ordered the settlers to create a general assembly. This body of government was known as the House of Burgesses. It made laws for the colony. The House of Burgesses also became a model for many future state legislatures in the United States.

Another important event in 1619 was the arrival of more women in Jamestown. Until this time, the only women in the colony were the wives of the earliest settlers and a few servants.

Servants Arrive in Colony

In August 1619, the first Africans came to North America. About 20 Africans were brought to Jamestown in a Dutch ship. The Africans were sold as servants in exchange for food supplies for the ship. They probably came from the west coast of Africa. Little history is written about them or their work in Jamestown. Historians believe some Africans were treated as slaves while other Africans were treated as **indentured servants**.

Many of the workers who arrived in Jamestown were indentured servants. These servants came to the colony to work for a certain number of years. In exchange for their labor, the servants received food and clothing. At the end of the time period, the workers were free to start their own life in the colony.

Many of the indentured servants hoped to buy land. They wanted to start a new life in the colony. Some of the indentured servants did well. Others did not grow rich because they did not have enough money to purchase land.

A Dutch ship arrived in Jamestown in 1619. This ship brought the first Africans to North America. These Africans were sold as servants.

Chapter Five

The End of Jamestown

The growing number of English settlements made the Powhatan Indians uneasy. By 1622, the Powhatan believed they might be losing their land. Many American Indians believed that the English were invaders. They decided to attack the plantations around Jamestown. In 1644, the Powhatan attacked again. Many people died in these fights.

The settlers and American Indians also fought over food supplies. Corn was an important crop in the area. Often, the settlers demanded that the American Indians trade or give up their corn supplies. When problems flared between the two groups, the settlers often destroyed the Indians' corn storage.

These actions hurt both groups' chances for staying alive.

American Indians grew concerned as the English built settlements outside of Jamestown.

Virginia Colony

The Virginia Colony was the first of many settlements the English built. Colonies were also built in Canada, Australia, and New Zealand.

Bacon's Rebellion

In 1676, Jamestown burned to the ground during a revolt. Nathaniel Bacon, a planter, led this fight. Bacon was a wealthy gentleman. He was also a relative, by marriage, of William Berkeley. Berkeley was governor of the Virginia Colony.

Bacon and the other colonists were angry with Governor Berkeley. They believed Berkeley could have stopped Indian attacks on settlements west of Jamestown. This revolt became known as Bacon's Rebellion.

During the rebellion, Bacon and his followers forced Berkeley to make changes to the colony.

In 1676, a fire destroyed Jamestown. The fire was started during a revolt led by Nathaniel Bacon. This revolt became known as Bacon's Rebellion.

The rebellion helped to lessen the power of the rich colonists. Taxes were cut for poor farmers. The power of Virginia's governor was lessened. The rebellion also made the colony more independent from England's king.

A New Capital

After the fire in 1676, the settlers rebuilt Jamestown. Jamestown served as the capital of the Virginia Colony for almost 100 years.

In 1698, Jamestown was struck by fire again. This time the colonists did not rebuild the city. The following year, the people of Virginia moved their capital to Williamsburg.

The city of Williamsburg was located 7 miles (11 kilometers) from Jamestown. Williamsburg was named for King William of England. The city served as the capital of the Virginia Colony until 1776.

Virginia Colony, mid-1600s

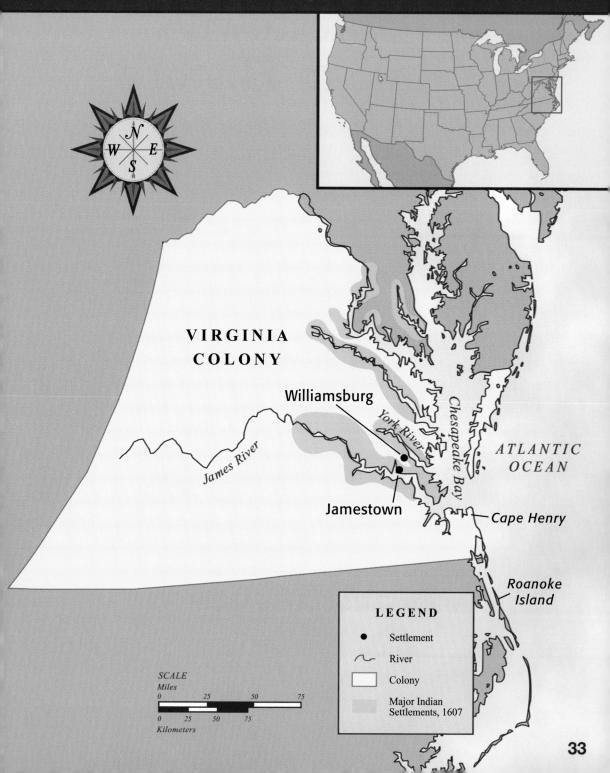

VIRGINIA
COLONY

Williamsburg

York River

James River

Chesapeake Bay

ATLANTIC
OCEAN

Jamestown

Cape Henry

Roanoke
Island

LEGEND

● Settlement

〰 River

▢ Colony

▢ Major Indian
Settlements, 1607

SCALE
Miles
0   25   50   75

0   25   50   75
Kilometers

Chapter Six

Jamestown's Role in History

Most of Jamestown's buildings rotted away after the settlers left the settlement. But the area continued to play small roles in American events. During the Revolutionary War (1775–1783), a military post was located there. During the Civil War (1861–1865), Confederate soldiers built a fort there. This fort helped keep the northern Union Army from moving along the James River.

Jamestown also made contributions to Virginia's state government. The House of Burgesses was the basis of the modern-day General Assembly of Virginia.

Pocahontas and John Smith are famous figures in American history. Both worked to save Jamestown. They are featured in stories, both fact and fiction.

Captain John Smith became an important figure in Virginia's history. Today, a statue of Smith stands in Jamestown, Virginia.

Keeping History Alive

Today, **archaeologists** and historians are studying the land where Jamestown once stood. They are searching for clues to Jamestown's history. Maps, charts, and old documents from the early days of Jamestown guide them in their search.

Many mysteries of Jamestown are now being solved. For nearly 200 years, historians believed that the original James Fort had washed into the James River. In 1994, archaeologists from

Archaeologists found this jug deep within the earth near Jamestown. This style of jug is known as Bartmann or "bearded man" because of the face that appears on the jug's neck.

Discovery of a Powhatan Village

In the early 1990s, Lynn Ripley found pieces of American Indian pottery on her property. She also found arrowheads. Ripley and her husband owned 300 acres (121 hectares) of land near the York River in Virginia.

Over the next 10 years, Ripley collected artifacts found on the property. In 2001, Ripley invited local archaeologists to view the artifacts. The archaeologists discovered that Ripley had helped to find the remains of the Powhatan village of Werowocomoco.

the Association for the Preservation of Virginia Antiquities (APVA) started digging in the area. Deep in the earth, they found two of the three walls from the fort. They also found hundreds of thousands of **artifacts** from the first half of the 1600s.

The team of archaeologists proved their find was James Fort. They studied documents that described how the fort was designed and built. Researchers also found a trash pit dating back to 1610–1611. On September 12, 1996, Virginia's

governor announced the discovery of this historic
site. The governor named it "James Fort Day."

In the summer of 2003, historians made
another important discovery. They found more clues
to James Fort's walls. This discovery showed that the
fort was much smaller. At first, archaeologists
believed James Fort covered an area of 1.75 acres
(.7 hectare). They now believe the fort only covered
an area of 1.1 acres (.4 hectare).

This lead doll is just one
of many interesting
items discovered at
Jamestown. Historians
believe an adult or child
may have owned this
doll. The doll may also
have been meant as an
item to trade to the
American Indians.

Clues to the Past

Thousands of interesting items have been dug up on dig sites in Jamestown. These artifacts date back to England and Europe in the 1500s and the 1600s. Discovered items have included metal curtain rings and drawer pulls. These items show that some of the colony's rich settlers brought furniture and drapes with them.

Candlesticks have also been found. The richer gentlemen probably could afford candles for light. Most people had to rely on the light from campfires or fireplaces.

Other objects found show that life for the early settlers was not all work. The settlers also enjoyed games. Archaeologists have found 12 gaming dice at Jamestown. The dice are very small, about the size of a pencil eraser.

Gaming dice

This is probably because dice games were illegal at Jamestown. Soldiers at the fort were not supposed to spend their time playing dice games. The players made their game pieces very small so they could be easily hidden.

Jamestown Today

Today, the APVA and the National Park Service manage the Jamestown area. Visitors can go to the site to learn about Jamestown. Guides give tours through the archaeological site and the laboratory. Tourists can also visit the area known as New Town. Here visitors learn about the town that grew outside the original fort.

The state of Virginia also operates Jamestown Settlement. This history museum features full-sized models of the *Susan Constant*, the *Godspeed*, and the *Discovery*. The site also has re-creations of James Fort and a Powhatan Indian village. Guides tell visitors about what life was like in the original Jamestown colony.

Each year, many tourists visit Jamestown Settlement. This living history museum shows visitors what life was like in Jamestown.

TIME LINE

Colonists build the
first English colony
in North America
on Roanoke Island.

King James I of England
grants a land charter to a
group of investors known
as the Virginia Company
of London.

Colonists run out
food during winter
this winter is called
the "starving time.

Roanoke Island
becomes the
Lost Colony.

| 1585 | 1587 | 1590 | 1606 | 1607 | 1609–1610 |

A new group of
colonists arrives on
Roanoke Island.

A group of 108
explorers sails up
the James River to
found Jamestown.

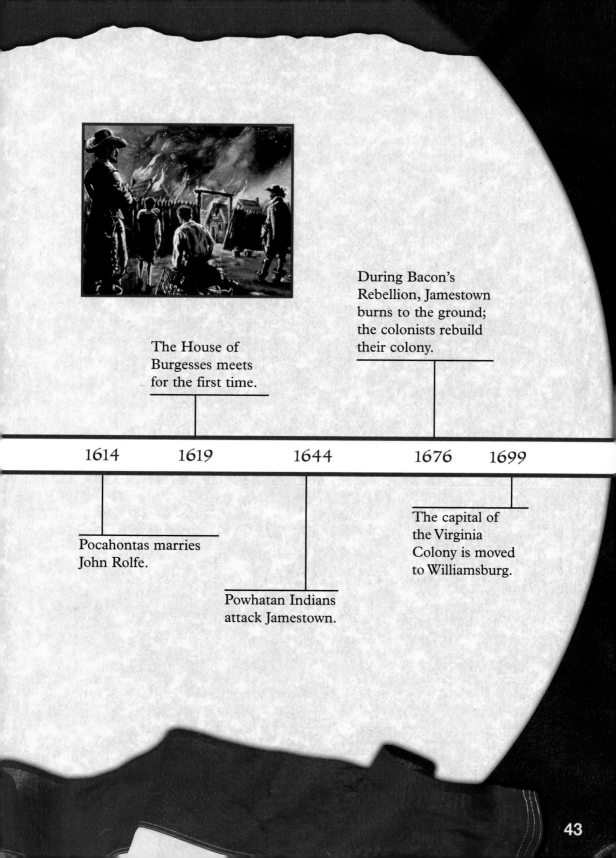

The House of
Burgesses meets
for the first time.

During Bacon's
Rebellion, Jamestown
burns to the ground;
the colonists rebuild
their colony.

| 1614 | 1619 | 1644 | 1676 | 1699 |

Pocahontas marries
John Rolfe.

The capital of
the Virginia
Colony is moved
to Williamsburg.

Powhatan Indians
attack Jamestown.

Glossary

archaeologist (ar-kee-OL-uh-jist)—a scientist who studies the life and cultures of the past

artifact (ART-uh-fakt)—an object made by human beings, especially a tool or weapon used in the past

charter (CHAR-tur)—a formal document that states the rights or duties of a group of people

confederacy (kuhn-FED-ur-uh-see)—a union of groups; Powhatan groups united under one government called the Powhatan Confederacy.

export (EK-sport)—products sold to other countries; tobacco was an important export for the Virginia Colony.

indentured servant (in-DEN-churd SUR-vuhnt)—someone who agrees to work for another person for a certain length of time in exchange for travel expenses, food, or housing

inquiry (IN-kwuh-ree)—an investigation

plantation (plan-TAY-shuhn)—a large farm found in warm areas where crops such as coffee, tea, tobacco, and cotton are grown

starve (STARV)—to suffer or die from lack of food

Read More

Boraas, Tracey. *The Powhatan: A Confederacy of Native American Tribes*. American Indian Nations. Mankato, Minn.: Bridgestone Books, 2003.

Dolan, Edward F. *The Lost Colony of Roanoke*. Kaleidoscope. New York: Benchmark Books/Marshall Cavendish, 2002.

January, Brendan. *The Jamestown Colony*. We The People. Minneapolis: Compass Point Books, 2001.

Marcovitz, Hal. *John Smith: Explorer and Colonial Leader*. Explorers of New Worlds. Philadelphia: Chelsea House, 2002.

Sonneborn, Liz. *Pocahontas, 1595–1617*. American Indian Biographies. Mankato, Minn.: Blue Earth Books, 2003.

Useful Addresses

APVA Jamestown Rediscovery
1367 Colonial Parkway
Jamestown, VA 23081
Visitors learn about the ongoing
digging and discoveries at the
Jamestown Rediscovery site.

Jamestown Settlement
Jamestown-Yorktown Foundation
P.O. Box 1607
Williamsburg, VA 23187–1607
A re-creation of the Jamestown
Colony takes visitors back in time
to the early 1600s. Visitors learn
firsthand what life was like in the
Jamestown Colony.

**The Powhatan Renape
Nation's American Indian
Heritage Museum**
Rankokus Indian Reservation
730 Rancocas Road
Mount Holly, NJ 08060
Visitors to this museum tour a
re-creation of a traditional
Powhatan village. The museum
also provides informational
exhibits featuring artifacts
and artwork.

Virginia Historical Society
428 North Boulevard
Richmond, VA 23220
The Virginia Historical Society's
museum provides information
about Virginia's earliest history,
including Roanoke Island and the
Jamestown Colony.

Internet Sites

FactHound offers a safe, fun way to find Internet sites related to this book. All of the sites on FactHound have been researched by our staff.

Here's how:
1. Visit *www.facthound.com*
2. Type in this special code **0736824626** for age-appropriate sites.
   Or enter a search word related to this book for a more general search.
3. Click on the **Fetch It** button.

FactHound will fetch the best sites for you!

Index